COMING
BACK TO
MY BODY

GEORGETTE NKWO

Editor: Bernice Angoh
Book Services by www.paperheartbook.com
Book Cover Photo: Nina Ara Lakota

COMING
BACK TO
MY BODY

This book is dedicated to Bernice, Dion-Albert, Sharon, Daryl, and Anderson. Thank you for being my mental, emotional, and spiritual shelter.

Table of Contents

Introduction

G rowing up, I spent time in hospitals and clinics at the direction of my father's friends who were doctors. This was usually after concierge consultation at home. These experiences sparked an interest in medicine. I was the child who everyone recognized as 'the one who got sick often.'

Something interesting happened during my 'sick" episodes: I maintained a healthy appetite, except for one occasion when I caught an aggressive type of malaria. The urgency in my mother's words and her hovering presence was heightened. Throughout all those childhood episodes, I became resilient. I bounced back each time. With my growth and understanding of the human body, I learned about the mental, emotional, physical, and spiritual aspects of the human condition. The most important lesson I learned was that the socioeconomic and political aspects of how the human body is governed affects us internally.

The way we experience the world is through our senses: sight, sound, taste, smell, touch, and intuition. All the senses require the human body to be at optimal functioning to experience the spectrum of sensations and feelings that make up the human experience. We would all agree that when one of the senses is not fully functioning, our bodies are forced to work differently.

In today's world of pollutants, externally and internally, also, self-induced, we can become detached from our bodies. What does this mean? We become unaware or unconscious in our way of life. The human brain is exceptional at reducing the energy it requires to perform tasks, and so it creates habits.

The way back to our bodies is to be intentional and have rituals.

This means awareness of why we do what we do. Dissociation--having an out of body experience-- is so common nowadays. Externally, we are bombarded with messages which conflict with the higher self, consequently we end up choosing the external sensations because it is easier.

CHAPTER 1

QI

The vital force of life whose flow must be unimpeded for good health

As an adult, if you asked anyone, I was the picture of vibrant, bouncy, colorful, physically active, and pure positivity. Over time, the above adjectives ceased to be true. Even I did not notice until the alarm bells started buzzing. I was dizzy, lightheaded, and nauseated all the time. I was losing weight and getting the compliments of a slender physique, yet it did not feel right. I confided in my siblings about the tension in my home and how it was physically affecting me. I received the support I could get which eased the overall malaise, but then it returned with additional force. At this point, I was done depending on Western Medicine to heal my heartache, and my physical complaints.

One morning, I woke up with an elevated heart rate and this sense of doom looming in the recesses of my mind. I googled acupuncture and found a Traditional Chinese Medicine clinic a few short miles from me. I drove there crying, not knowing how or why. The check-in nurse asked the usual questions and then asked what brought me in. The slow trickle of tears became a waterfall punctuated by sounds of me saying, "I don't feel good, I just don't feel good, I don't know, but I know I don't feel good."

Dark pixie cut, petite and oozing concern, the doctor in her Chinese accent said, "Don't worry, I fix you." I mentioned her accent and ethnicity because those words stayed with me. Those words were a reminder that there was hope and I was not alone. She then asked a series of questions and examined my tongue. My Qi was blocked. I heard the word Qi and my nerdy brain perked up. You see, the only exposure to the word Qi was through movies. Qi is usually portrayed as this light in the middle of your chest which you get to summon, tap into, or exude. Sometimes it is portrayed as a ball of light that is manipulated with the hands, or a sphere of light which surrounds you. I explained to the doctor that I was a nurse who grew up with African homeopathy, and that I wanted to understand what she was treating. She gladly explained that Qi was the life force.

It had an electrical, chemical/hormonal, and temperature quality which when blocked affects the organs.

My pulse was weak and thready, my thyroid was blocked, she went on and on. What caught my attention was when she mentioned my lung Qi was blocked. My brain came alive again and asked what it meant. The doctor said, I was carrying grief around. I chuckled and told her, I was not depressed, sad, or grieving anything. In fact, apart from my body feeling like it was falling apart, I was happy and happy and in good cheer. She leaned her head to the side and said, "No honey, it's not about sadness, it's deeper than that." She proceeded to stick the needles in my arms, legs, midsection, and the top of my head. Instructions were provided and I laid there in the quiet room, staring at the stained ceiling tiles. I noticed the smell of burning incense, somewhere, the heater went on and off, the creaking sounds of someone pulling their chair back and then my floating mind returned to the room I was in. I wondered about the charts on the wall in Chinese with illustrations of all the pressure points in the body. Slowly, I drifted into sleep, with moments of wakefulness in between, but then returning to silence.

I woke up as the doctor was taking out the pins in my legs. She was pleasant and asked me how I liked my nap. *Nap? How long was I asleep?* Trying to get my bearings straight, the doctor replied to my inaudible question, "You were asleep for an hour." She reassessed my tongue and noted that some color had come back to it. She seemed pleased.

Holding both of my wrists, she said my pulse was still weak but had slightly improved. While she jauntily talked about the plan for treatment, I noticed I felt rested. Better than I had had in a year. Instructions included drinking water often and going home to rest. She gave me some herbs and suggested a few teas to drink. Getting off the table, I felt physically lighter and suddenly hungry. *What a feeling!* I thought to myself, *maybe this is the cure.*

On my way home, I felt untethered, like I was floating; like an astronaut disconnected from the spacecraft. That image made me smile. What do I know about the feeling of space? I watched fearfully yet curiously and in awe of how light my body felt. The hairs on my arms tingled. My nausea had vanished.

I realized that what I called stress was really anxiety riddling my mind and body.

That anxiety in turn had weakened my lungs. My heart was heavy, yet I felt free—it was the most unusual feeling.

After the longest nap I could remember in years, I felt hunger pangs. When I ate, I ate slowly. My thoughts were not racing, so I leaned into the quietness of my brain. This was new for me. As I took a deep breath, the lump in my throat and chest-- that I had felt but did not mention to the doctor--seemed to have disappeared. This untethered floaty feeling was nice.

As the day wore on, I leaned in to hug my child and did not feel anything. I watched my mother chatter away on the phone, and I felt nothing. I spoke to a friend and felt distant. I tried to catch up with work and prepare for the next day and felt disengaged. Oh no! I was untethered and floating with no emotions whatsoever, yet I summoned fear. Given the various time zones my sisters were living in, I could not wake anyone from sleep to tell them I was afraid. So, I called a close friend and told them my fears of not feeling anything and being disengaged. After the words left my mouth, more fear popped up, what if he judges me, thinks I have lost my mind, or that something was severely wrong with me? As his voice faded into my loud thoughts, additional fear set in. I couldn't focus long enough to continue the conversation I started. Then suddenly, I heard my name loudly through the phone. "Are you okay? are you there?" I paused and then responded. The conversation that ensued was nothing I could have ever prayed for or manifested. The outpouring of attention, support, and hope I received from my friend was unparalleled. The suggestions I received were to journal how I was feeling and call as often as I needed to.

HOW I CAME BACK TO MYSELF:

- I recognized that something was wrong.

- I listened to my intuition and acted on it.

- I used my voice to speak up and started healing with curiosity.

What is your intuition telling you right now about your physical, emotional, and psychological state of being?

**Write about a time you listened to your intuition
and how it benefitted you.**

**Do you remember a time when you did not listen to your intuition?
Share below.**

Do you struggle with taking inspired action? Why?
What can you do to fix it?

_____

_____

_____

_____

_____

_____

_____

_____

_____

_____

_____

_____

_____

_____

_____

_____

_____

_____

_____

_____

_____

_____

_____

_____

_____

CHAPTER 2

GRIEF

A spiritual journey of the heart and soul

As hesitant as I can be to rely on technology, my nurse brain went into overdrive, and I dove into the rabbit hole of the internet scouring for peer reviewed articles on acupuncture and Qi. Anatomy and physiology, dermatomes, neural pathways, connection of organs and physical manifestations of complex emotional and mental states. I was especially interested in the mind-body connection. Intellectually, I knew this, but to read scholarly articles about it was mind blowing. I discovered that body parts which anatomically have mechanical functions also have emotional responses.

After a couple of weeks of this newfound comprehension, grief became more present. In nursing school, we were taught the five stages of grief: denial, anger, bargaining, depression, and acceptance. I thought to myself, where on this spectrum do I fall into?

I soon learned that resentment is part of grief. That grief is not linear in expression within space and time and mine was embedded in ambient stress as well. Through journaling, I started to really connect the dots and go as far back and out as I could to remember if I had unmet needs, unspoken words, and unfinished conversations. Guess what? There was a little of everything. Things I had logged into the past, that no longer needed to be addressed, or could not be addressed because too much time had passed. That untethered floaty feeling disappeared, and I was bound once again to the harsh reality of emotional pain.

I journaled throughout the day until I could not recognize my handwriting. I emptied out my head and heart and spoke the words that were unsaid, finished the conversations that were unfinished and forgave myself and everyone, perceived or real, who hurt me, or who I hurt. I journaled mostly about my symptoms, feelings, and emotions. This helped me to become more transparent, vulnerable, and provided me with added knowledge to understand my body.

During my third acupuncture session, the Chinese doctor mentioned I should check for uterine fibroids. Once again, I scoured the internet for medical journals and absorbed all the information on fibroids. Ayurvedic practices were common conversations with my sisters but this time, I dug a little deeper. As I continued these conversations, the Doshas seemed to explain what was going on in my body. I also learned a lot more about Chakras.

Ayurveda is the knowledge of life, a system of medicine dated thousands of years in India. This form of medicine parallels balancing the Qi. Their approaches are different, but the outcomes are the same. Chakras-are the wheels of energy points in the body that must stay open and aligned, like Qi in flow. Chakras affect the emotional, physical, and spiritual self. Doshas are part of Ayurveda. Dosha is defined as a combination of bio-energies that describe your tendencies and physical nature. Reading and studying about ancient treatments, as I studied my body and tried all the herbs and concoctions available, shed light on how my body worked and responded to anything I consumed. I grieved the loss of the past as it gave me new understanding of who I was. As I journaled about my grief and talked about it with my trusted friend and siblings, the untethered floaty feeling slowly returned.

HOW I CAME BACK
TO MY BODY:

- I Journaled about my symptoms, feelings, and emotions.

- I started learning how to be transparent and vulnerable.

- I added knowledge of other ways to understand my body by reading and listening to audio books on specific topics of interest.

Do you have an outlet for your emotions and feelings?
What things do you do?

_____

_____

_____

_____

_____

_____

_____

_____

_____

_____

_____

_____

_____

_____

_____

_____

_____

_____

_____

_____

_____

_____

_____

_____

_____

_____

_____

Do you struggle with being vulnerable? Write down a time when you were the most vulnerable. How did it feel?

What do you do to actively learn more about your body and mind?

_____

_____

_____

_____

_____

_____

_____

_____

_____

_____

_____

_____

_____

_____

_____

_____

_____

_____

_____

_____

_____

_____

What spiritual practices keep you grounded and balanced?

CHAPTER 3

LOSS

An opening, a clearing or cleansing of energy to make way for new energy

In the spirit of finding newness and navigating the grief process, I found myself in disagreement with my mother over several things. Some may say, it is a rite of passage for adult daughters with their mothers. I say, it was that, but it was also a "getting to know myself better."

I developed a new vocabulary in my quest for peace. What happened next was an exacerbation of loss, anxiety, and alienation. During a subsequent acupuncture visit, as the needles were being placed, I became nauseous, short of breath and started shaking uncontrollably. Two doctors and a nurse gently held me in place to prevent me from falling off the table. Just then, I felt a needle on the top of my lip. Within seconds, all the shaking stopped, and I was lying still again. I was offered a ginger drink and an extra thirty minutes of treatment. The doctor said I had a panic attack and that I needed to see my primary care physician for additional medical testing.

At the women's clinic, I was diagnosed with fibroids and the first treatment offered was a hysterectomy. I vehemently refused it. My brain chatter immediately mocked me for feeling confident again. The rumination about the new diagnosis was crippling. I found a therapist and started talk therapy.

Therapy was new and it took away the stress I associated with healing myself emotionally. It freed my mind to tackle the new diagnosis. I went back to my African herbs and concoctions. Some of the herbs were familiar and others I began to learn about in detail. The teas significantly improved hormonal symptoms and the untethered floaty feeling returned. My Qi once again was flowing.

This time, I rested in the lightness and airiness of it. I was not disengaged emotionally or mentally. I removed dairy, meat, bread, and sweets, in increments and slowly added them back eventually. What I learned during this time was loss; the loss of normalcy in my body and the loss of how I related to my immediate surroundings. I even lost connection with my friends. I was developing a new language surrounding who I was and that began with the loss of my friends. It made me sad and angry. I tried to lean into the untethered floaty feeling to bring myself back to some semblance of acceptance, but the more I leaned into the lightness, the more distant I grew from my friends and family.

I talked harshly about cutting people off and just going off the grid to sustain myself because of my discoveries into the food industry. It was heartbreaking to realize how hopeless it was to truly eat a living diet.

I soon learned that with awareness comes isolation.

The loneliness grew, and I struggled to socialize. My core belief system was present, yet I could feel my body changing. I could feel my heart and mind changing. For this reason, I named my coaching practice, EVOLVEFULNESS ™. I was a caterpillar evolving into its fullness.

I was shedding an old belief system about my body and who had sovereignty over it. I was shedding the idea of loving people hard, doing the right thing without question, allowing others to invade my mental and emotional space, all in the name of love.

This is why so many things were unfinished in the past.

HOW I CAME BACK TO MY BODY:

- As I continued to journal, I acknowledged that emotionally barring one person out of my life affected my expression of love for others.

- I learned what boundaries were and how to create them for myself.

- I learned to always ask what people want before I swoop in to help them.

- I learned how to ask for my needs to be met--I don't know any mind readers, so that one was huge for me.

- I learned to listen with my heart and keep it open so that feelings could flow freely in and out, and not cause blockages in my body.

- I learned that peace within was priceless.

Do you have good boundaries with the people in your life?
With whom do you have the least boundaries with and why?

_____

_____

_____

_____

_____

_____

_____

_____

_____

_____

_____

_____

_____

_____

_____

_____

_____

_____

_____

_____

_____

_____

When you tell people "No" how does it make you feel?
Why do you think it makes you feel that way?

Are you carrying any grief around? If yes, what is it,
and what is stopping you from letting it go?

_____

_____

_____

_____

_____

_____

_____

_____

_____

_____

_____

_____

_____

_____

_____

_____

_____

_____

_____

_____

_____

_____

_____

_____

What is the biggest loss you've ever suffered?
How did it change you?

CHAPTER 4

SURRENDER

Releasing attachment to struggles, obstacles and challenges & acceptance of what current reality is.

In the weeks that followed my diagnosis, I went through some grueling medical testing and received multiple blood and iron transfusions. I learned about the vitamins, minerals, and enzymes that were building blocks for gut health, which transported finished products to the brain. The mind-body, gut-brain connection was apparent in my everyday life. My good friend and sisters held my hand through the medical saga. The outpouring of love and care from the community I was growing was nice. I learned to surrender. Not give up, surrender.

I allowed what was happening to happen and experienced all my emotions. There was a sense of relief from knowing what was making me sick. There was joy in that being a nurse, I understood the treatment plan. There was confidence that all the modalities, Ayurveda, Acupuncture, African herbalism, played a part in me returning to my body.

Surrender removed all the "should have" in my life.

1. I should have unmatched physical support.

2. I should have the money.

3. I should be mother of the year through all of this.

4. I should mind my mother and her needs.

5. I should still be able to work as if I was not falling apart medically.

Surrender afforded me the confidence to ask for my needs to be met by my friends, family, and my job. Behold, all the core needs I asked for were met. I became bolder. Whoo-hoo! If you knew me, I was already bold. I occupied space when I could.

This surrender came with a healthy dose of humility. It was harder than I imagined, and I learned to be like water.

HOW I CAME BACK TO MY BODY:

- Accept help.

- Feel my feelings.

- Participate actively in my medical care.

How easy is it for you to ask for help? When was the last time you asked for help? What kind of help did you need and what was the feedback?

_____

_____

_____

_____

_____

_____

_____

_____

_____

_____

_____

_____

_____

_____

_____

_____

_____

_____

_____

_____

_____

_____

_____

_____

Do you equate asking for help with the feeling of laziness? Why?
If yes, what subconscious programming led you to this belief?

Write down an incident when surrendering was beneficial to you.

CHAPTER 5

GRATITUDE

Seeing the value in everything, and that everything will be a benefit in the end.

Surgery to remove the fibroids, myomectomy, was planned and executed flawlessly. While hospitalized, the night staff was wonderful. I was treated with respect and dignity. They were attentive and my needs were met. Usually, I throw around the nurse title but this time I did not. This was true surrender.

I am usually the nurse giving care and this time, I had to learn how to receive, and that was new to me too. I was happy to be alive and wasn't afraid to say aloud what I was grateful for. I got in the habit of looking for the positive aspect with each bump in the recovery process.

My sisters and my friend were raw and sore with concern since I went through surgery, and my hospital, stay alone. With continued encouragement from friends, now catching on to my medical saga, the support grew. I spent a week by myself after surgery—gladly a friend had kept my child during that time. When he returned, I saw that that he was more responsible than I ever gave him credit for. He was very attentive and observant. He refused to go stay with an aunt or his father and chose to heal with me during that summer. I was incredibly grateful to have him by my side.

I practiced surrender with my child by allowing him to do the challenging and difficult things for me like turning on the stove to make tea and cutting vegetables with the big scary knife. I laugh now but I held my breath then. We had talked about doing difficult things safely prior to surgery. He took it to heart and embodied the sentiment. Church ladies showed up with food, neighbors stopped by to check on me, my office manager and supervisor came with food as well and spent some time with me. With an attitude of gratitude, all fear was lost, and stress seemed to melt away in those moments. Steadily, love and peace over-flowed. Socialization was new again. It required effort on my part, but I began reconnecting with the community I almost gave up on.

I was even grateful for the hardships that came my way because I approached all kinds of relationships differently. With more compassion, empathy, and an even stronger desire to right any wrongs that lingered. The societal boxes I put myself and others in melted away.

I created boundaries, not walls, new perspectives, not judgements, and new hopes, not fears.

The practice of gratitude made me see myself kindly, more lovingly, and more compassionately. Love for myself became easier to express and easier to pour into others. The practice of gratitude improved the mind-body connection.

HOW I CAME BACK TO MY BODY:

- I woke up daily with gratitude.

- I made a detailed list of everything for which I was grateful.

- Socialization gave me rest. The kind of rest sleep does not provide.

- Grace

In line with gratitude, I experienced what Grace meant. As humans, we rely heavily on Grace to be given to us based on merit.

What I learned was that I could give myself Grace in unmeasurable amounts.

In bushels, yards, football stadiums full, Grace from the entire universe! It was all mine to give to myself as much as I gave to others. To allow myself to step back and rest, remembering the awe and wonder of the untethered floaty feeling. Grief, loss, and gratitude could be a shedding of an old belief system.

- I gave myself the rest and forgiveness I needed.

- I gave grace to friends and family.

- In stuck moments, I paused and surrendered.

What is something you haven't forgiven yourself for?

What are the top three things you're most grateful for?

_____

_____

_____

_____

_____

_____

_____

_____

_____

_____

_____

_____

_____

_____

_____

_____

_____

_____

_____

_____

When was the last time you experienced grace?
Write about it below.

_____

_____

_____

_____

_____

_____

_____

_____

_____

_____

_____

_____

_____

_____

_____

_____

_____

_____

_____

_____

_____

_____

_____

_____

_____

_____

CHAPTER 6

MOVEMENT

Connecting to Spirit on a more universal and divine level.

Six weeks after surgery I was cleared to resume activities as tolerated. My nurse-brain understood the instructions clearly, but I interpreted it as "you can resume running." In timely fashion, family and friends warned me jokingly to sit down and heal, but moving my body is how I gauge my health and fitness. My goal is always to balance my desire for movement while paying attention to the cues my body was sending.

I started walking when I could, and eliminated the idea that as a runner I should bounce back quickly. Couch to 5k, I told myself. I walked. I documented it.

Within five weeks, I resumed yoga. This time, intentionally. I felt my joints moving again with renewed strength. I noticed my breath go through my lungs and expand my belly as I inhaled and contracted as I exhaled. Every twist was met with caution, but it was joyous and enjoyable. I could move my body again without dizziness or soreness.

Minding my body mechanics during chores seemed like a dance to avoid injury, but I smiled through it all. With every stretch, I reminded myself that I had sovereignty over my body, my thoughts, and my feelings. I practiced mindful and intentional movements with breathwork. Qigong. Qigong is a combination of meditation, breathing and movement to heal the body. I breathed through panic attacks and took cold showers to restore balance. I practiced my breath work during acupuncture and all through the western treatment of my fibroids.

As I continued to learn about my body and create new habits and rituals, I came across the word pranayama. Pranayama is a yogic breathing exercise to harness energy. Healing the body requires a healthy dose of movement. I shined as I returned home to my body.

HOW I CAME BACK
TO MY BODY:

- Yoga

- Qigong

- Pranayama

- Walking

- Being intentional while doing chores.

What moves you the most about life?

What new forms of movement would you like to try for the next 21 days? How will this impact your mind and body?

CHAPTER 7

SLEEP

*Accessing vital spiritual and physical
instructions needed for
optimal function of the body.*

For a few years, my nights were interrupted with sweating and panic. On top of that, the fear and anxiety of not getting enough sleep was even more crippling.

As a child, I was called "sleeping beauty," and for many years that was my superpower. I slept all the time and anywhere. So, for me to have lost that superpower as an adult was not acceptable. To fix this, I started a sleep hygiene practice which included the right foods for me before bedtime and no electronics one hour before bedtime. The electronics part is still a work in progress. However, my sleep routine improved, and I started sleeping through the night.

I still wake up at night sometimes, but those occurrences continue to be short-lived and less stressful. The mental clarity, emotional, and mental stability which ensued because of my new habits was refreshing: no panic attacks and no anxiety during the day--except for those phone calls when a supervisor asks you to see them in their office. My skin cleared up, my complexion was smoother, and I looked rested. I learned how to take decent naps again.

The quality of your day is determined by what you do in the first two hours after you wake up. What do your first two hours look like? What can you do to change or adjust it to make it more beneficial to you?

HOW I CAME BACK
TO MY BODY:

- I go to sleep at a reasonable hour at night.

- I prioritize stillness during the first few minutes of my morning.

- I meditate- it's considered movement or physical exercise.

- I stay hydrated: Water, then tea/coffee or fruits with high water content.

How much sunlight do you get during the day? What have you learned about the correlation between sunlight and Vitamin D?

_____

_____

_____

_____

_____

_____

_____

_____

_____

_____

_____

_____

_____

_____

_____

_____

_____

_____

_____

_____

_____

_____

_____

What new habit would you like to incorporate into the first few hours of your day? List them below.

_____

_____

_____

_____

_____

_____

_____

_____

_____

_____

_____

_____

_____

_____

_____

_____

_____

_____

_____

_____

_____

_____

_____

_____

CHAPTER 8

MEDITATION

Connecting to the Source of Love.

Meditation is a practice that has existed for millennia. It is the practice of bringing oneself into awareness. The first step of getting into meditation is learning to keep the body still. Just like any new habit, this can be done incrementally. Sit or lie still for one minute and increase the time gradually. Once getting into stillness is doable, add guided meditation and get comfortable with it.

You can access good, guided meditations on YouTube, Soundcloud, in yoga settings or on certain podcasts.

The outcome of meditation depends on the intention set before the practice.

For instance, when I wake up with an elevated heart rate, and find my brain moving faster than my body, I can set an intention to slow down and retain my energy, or slow down and let go of the energy.

As much as a large group of the practicing population meditate in the mornings, meditation can be done anytime during the day, even in the middle of a busy train station. Granted, being still in chaos is what we all aspire to be. Wouldn't it be amazing to quiet the mind and be still outside of the comfort of quiet spaces? It may be challenging but it is possible.

Practicing meditation enabled me to get closer to my higher self.

The spiritual self. During this practice, which was guided most of the time, I learned to find the untethered floaty feeling, to induce it, and rest in it. This means, the brain chatter became a part of the practice, not necessarily the interrupter of the practice. I learned to listen to my emotions and brain chatter, to stop fighting them and instead observe them. Meditation is a grounding practice when combined with pranayama or Qigong. It brings all the energies of the emotions into balance. For me, my morning routine seems incomplete without meditation, however, this can be practiced throughout the day.

HOW I CAME BACK TO MYSELF:

- I learned to give myself me-time.

- I learned that prioritizing my peace of mind and sanity wasn't selfish.

- I became intentional with everything I did.

Do you feel guilty about putting yourself first? If yes, why?

When was the last time you prioritized yourself?
What did you do? How did it feel?

CHAPTER 9

FOOD

The bridge between man's spirit
and his body

As I mentioned before, when I was cautious about everything while trying to heal my body I lost weight, but I did not feel good. I received compliments for my looks, but I did not like how I looked. My body composition, its bone structure, fat deposits and genetics dictated that the weight loss I achieved did not benefit me at that point.

My African genetics allowed for my chest and backside to be full without effort, so the weight at which I was at that point was not healthy for me.

I began a new and healthy relationship with food. A relationship with food where I was aware that food was medicine as well as a source of fuel and pleasure. I slowly gained weight as I continued to move my body back to where I felt healthy again.

Being physically beautiful is a wonderful feeling but feeling beautiful on the inside as well brings even more confidence, and vibrancy to life.

Food carries metaphysical energy and spiritual energy. The word metaphysical has jumped from the science realm into mainstream conversations as well. It means, outside of the human perception. Food experts talk about the nutritional benefits of food which is excellent. However, there is more to food that meets the five physical senses. Foods from the earth carries higher vibrational energy therefore, it is best for human consumption.

Food from the earth will place you in rest and digest which sharpens your five senses and your intuition. Have you noticed that when you cook while relaxed, the food is cooked well and generally more satisfying even with a smaller than usual portion? Praying before meals is a grounding exercise to place your body in relaxation and gratitude. Processed foods carry a low vibrational energy which tends to lead to modern diseases. In ancient times, from religious texts and other secular practices, food was used for rituals because of their metaphysical properties.

When this perspective became clear to me, my belief system evolved into one of honoring myself.

HOW I CAME BACK TO MY BODY:

- I changed my thoughts about food.

- I started to see food as more than just fuel for the body. Food became a way to celebrate my body.

- I used food as a tool of self-compassion.

CHAPTER 10

GRACE

Receiving loving-kindness
just at the right time.

Ａs I find myself reclaiming sovereignty over my body, I reclaim my power as the co-creator of my destiny.

The body is a conduit through which the intangibles in life are expressed.

Beauty, joy, love, and even negative feelings.

Sovereignty over oneself is an intentional intrinsic agreement with all the parts of who we are and who we choose to grow into.

As described, stacking good habits, or staggering them with each other provided the solutions to heal. Creating rituals is about being intentional about the habits and how they are practiced. By so doing, we can create several pathways to lean on when we fall out of balance. It is okay to enjoy the pathways you create as well as the process. The untethered floaty-feeling I found became an energy I could linger in. It also brought me back to center--freedom.

We get out of balance from time to time. Even as an adult, my family trembles when I fall ill but their confidence in me coming out on the other side is much stronger. My appetite remains healthy and continues to transcend into an appetite for the full experience of who I am.

Fear is a guardian.

Make peace with fear, loss, and grief so you can greet, surrender, curiosity, grace, and gratitude as they create paths back to your body. I am home.

HOW I CAME BACK TO MY BODY:

- I stopped being too hard on myself.

- I learned to give myself the same compassion I extended to others.

- I started to see every shortcoming and obstacle as a moment of Grace.

What does Grace mean to you?

How do you recognize when to give yourself Grace?

How do you give Grace to others?

"Stop playing small.

You are the universe in
ecstatic motion."

- R U M I

7-DAY JUMPSTART

Welcome to my seven-day jumpstart program. This program is designed to increase your energy levels while cleansing the body. It involves significantly eating more vegetables and fruits: foods from the earth. However, I have curated the program for you to maintain stable blood sugar levels, while getting the benefits of increased energy.

We are constantly bombarded with environmental toxins, as well as toxins consumed in artificial sweeteners, food additives, our medications, and chemicals we use in our hair and skin. On top of this, undesirable bacteria in our guts can produce toxins as well, which can enter the blood stream.

Our gut health is directly connected to our brain health. When the gut is out of balance, it affects our mood, digestion, sleep, and even processing of medications.

HOW DOES THIS JUMPSTART PLAN WORK?

The 7-Day Jumpstart plan is a detox plan, and it works to encourage three phases of natural detoxification in the body.

- Some of the best foods to eat on a detox include proteins, B Vitamins, Vitamin E and C, magnesium, selenium, and zinc.

- The first thing to increase in your diet during the detox program is fiber because it supports healthy elimination of waste from the bowel. Stagnant waste in the bowel re-absorbs toxins. Eating a wide variety of vegetables provides good fiber for proper elimination of waste.

- Drink plenty of water which helps to flush out waste from your kidneys. This could include a teaspoon of lime in warm water during the jumpstart to lubricate the gastrointestinal tract for easy digestion and removal of accumulated mucus.

LET'S DIVE IN!

Below is a sample diet plan to guide you on how to eat during the 7-day jumpstart program. All ingredients can be adjusted according to taste, but the key components are increased consumption of vegetables and other forms of fiber and hydration.

DAY 1

BREAKFAST

Oatmeal with cinnamon sweetened with berries or agave nectar or honey.

OR avocado toast, with a slice of tomatoes and boiled/fried eggs

NOTE

Oatmeal releases glucose slowly in the body and cinnamon helps to lower fasting blood glucose levels. The berries, agave nectar, and honey have a low glycemic index which means they easily break down to give you energy and keep your blood sugar in check. Avocadoes are rich in healthy fats to keep you full longer.

LUNCH

Add steamed or baked vegetables to beans, lentils, peas, and baked or steamed meat. Example: Black bean enchiladas.

All the above have a low glycemic index and will fill you up. Feel free to look up recipes that you like.

DINNER

Mac and cheese! plain.

OR baked fish dinner like salmon over rice with a side of roasted vegetables

It is filling enough that any snack after dinner, which could also be a yoghurt and nuts, will not increase your blood sugar levels. This will improve sleep and prevent you from waking up too hungry in the morning.

DAY 2

BREAKFAST

You can eat the same thing as the day before or have eggs with spinach, onions and all the fixings. Use herbs for seasoning. Add a slice of fruit and toasted whole wheat bread.

NOTE

This is also a low glycemic index breakfast. The healthy fats in eggs decrease inflammation in the body. Inflammation is one of the reasons weight-loss is difficult. Also, it will keep you full until lunchtime.

LUNCH

A salad with salmon or grilled chicken. Use salad dressing sparingly and no croutons.

NOTE

The greens in the salad must be leafy. Iceberg lettuce has no nutritional value.

DINNER

Add vegetables and lean meat (not fried). Your carbs could be legumes, like lunch from the previous day. Refer to your list of snacks if you need one before bedtime.

DAY 3

BREAKFAST

Fruit smoothie! Add kale or spinach.

NOTE

You can add Greek yogurt for protein. Use natural sweeteners like honey or agave nectar. You can use orange juice (no added sugar) to sweeten it.

LUNCH

Tuna salad sandwich on whole wheat or sprouted bread, ham or turkey sandwich on whole wheat or sprouted bread. Feel free to load up on veggies. Instead of chips, opt for fruit slices or a side salad.

NOTE

If you opt for the side salad, do not add croutons or shredded cheese because your sandwich bread has all the carbs you need. Also, wheat bread has a low glycemic index.

DINNER

Eat left over dinners or opt for a stir-fry with lots of vegetables and a smaller serving of pasta.

DAY 4

BREAKFAST

Banana pancakes. Add fruit and add a natural sweetener like honey, 100% amber grade maple syrup or agave nectar. Add fruits. You can always refer to the previous breakfast choices.

NOTE

This breakfast is sure to make you happy and you can mix and match with toasted nuts as well.

LUNCH

Chili without chips or cornbread. Load the chili with beans and other legumes. Spicy chicken tomato chickpea soup or low salt soups with meat in it.

NOTE

Chili is a one-stop-shop for a balanced meal if you load it with legumes. Soups can also be filling.

DINNER

Stir-fry chicken and pasta add vegetables. Or recipes that call for lots of vegetables with pasta. You can bake tilapia or catfish as your protein.

**Enjoy dinner as you are in the middle of the jumpstart program and starting to feel overall better.

DAY 5

BREAKFAST

Boiled or lightly fried whole egg or egg whites. Add a smoothie with kale or spinach in it. If bread is necessary, toasted wheat bread or sprouted bread is better.

NOTE

Low glycemic index especially with the egg whites.

LUNCH

Instant pot roast, use brown rice or grilled shrimp salad, no croutons.

NOTE

Pot roast tends to be comfort food for many but substitute your comfort food here with no shredded cheese or excess grease.

DINNER

Italian meatballs, with a small serving size of pasta of your choice. Add vegetables on the side.

NOTE

The meatballs would fill you up especially if you had a salad for lunch. Use nighttime snack list as a guide.

DAY 6

BREAKFAST
Any variation of the previous breakfasts

LUNCH
Any variation of the previous lunches

DINNER
Any variation of the previous dinners and refer to your healthy snack list.

DAY 7

BREAKFAST

Fruit and veggie smoothie. Add superfoods like chia seeds, matcha, cacao, hemp seeds. Or add grains and fruit to your pancakes or top the pancakes with them.

NOTE

Cacao is the least processed version of cocoa powder. This breakfast is sweet and sure to make you ready for the day.

LUNCH

Baked fish or shrimp or seafood in general with lots of vegetables. For carbs, it must be a small serving of pasta, rice, or a bed of legumes.

DINNER

Stir-fry with lots of vegetables.

Sample Recipe 1

Creamy Tomato Soup Recipe

Our go-to creamy tomato soup recipe. Adding parmesan and heavy cream makes it so satisfying and balances the acidity. It's also a quick and easy 30-minute soup that keeps well in the fridge.

INGREDIENTS

- 4 Tbsp unsalted butter

- 2 yellow onions, (3 cups finely chopped)

- 3 garlic cloves, (1 Tbsp minced)

- 56 oz crushed tomatoes, (two, 28-oz cans) with their juice, preferably San Marzano

- 2 cups chicken stock

- 1/4 cup chopped fresh basil, plus more to serve.

- 1 Tbsp sugar, or added to taste.

- 1/2 tsp black pepper, or to taste.

- 1/2 cup heavy whipping cream, or to taste to combat acidity.

- 1/3 cup parmesan cheese, freshly grated, plus more to serve.

INSTRUCTIONS

1. Heat a nonreactive pot or enameled Dutch oven over medium heat. Add butter then add chopped onions. Sauté 10-12 minutes, stirring occasionally, until softened and golden. Add minced garlic and sauté for 1 minute until fragrant.

2. Add crushed tomatoes with their juice, chicken stock, chopped basil, sugar (or add sugar to taste), and black pepper. Stir together and bring to a boil then reduce heat, partially cover with lid and simmer for 10 minutes.

3. You can leave your soup with a chunky consistency, but if you like a blended/creamy soup, use an immersion blender to blend the soup in the pot to desired consistency or transfer to a blender in batches and blend until smooth (being careful not to over-fill the blender with hot liquid), then return blended soup to the pot over medium heat.

4. Add 1/2 cup heavy cream, 1/3 cup freshly grated parmesan cheese and return to a simmer. Season to taste with salt and pepper if needed and turn off the heat. *

5. Ladle into warm bowls and top with more parmesan and chopped fresh basil.

Sample recipe 2

Salmon wrap

INGREDIENTS

SALMON

- 14oz/400g salmon, in cubes
- Salt and pepper
- 1 tbsp olive oil
- 1 tbsp lemon juice

SALAD

- 2 cucumbers
- 2 tomatoes
- 1/2 avocado
- 2 scallions
- 2 1/2 cups salad greens
- 1 cup herbs and arugula chopped - mint and basil.
- Salt, pepper, lemon juice olive oil

TZATZIKI

- 1 cup yogurt
- 1-2 garlic clove
- 1 tbsp dill thinly chopped.
- 1/2 cup cucumbers thinly chopped.

ADDITIONALLY:

- Salt and pepper
- 5-6 pitted, chopped olives.
- 4 gluten free tortillas

INSTRUCTIONS

1. Preheat oven to 350F/180C. Chop the salmon filets into bite-sized pieces. spread in a single layer over a baking sheet lined with parchment paper for an easier clean-up. Drizzle olive oil, lemon juice, salt, and pepper and bake for about 12-15 minutes or until golden brown.

2. Chop the cucumber and dill for the tzatziki thinly, then mix with garlic, yogurt, and salt in a small bowl.

3. Chop the salad vegetables. Add all ingredients for the salad into a bowl and toss!

4. Place some of the salmon, tzatziki and salad onto a tortilla, sprinkle chopped olives and wrap.

5. Enjoy immediately.

NOTES

*To meal prep this recipe, you can make the tzatziki and salmon ahead (they will be good for 3-4 days in the fridge). If you also want to make a meal prep a salad you can make some cabbage, some olives, jalapeno and use some whole cherry tomatoes. Remember to keep all the parts for the wrap separately - either in airtight compartment containers or each individually packed in an airtight container in the fridge.

**Another salad you can try:

- 2 cucumbers, chopped.

- ⅓ cup olives

- 2 tbsp pickled jalapeno slices (optional)

- 4 tbsp parsley thinly chopped.

- 1 garlic clove, minced.

- 1 large ripe avocado

- 1 cup arugula

- ½ lemon, juice of

- 1 tsp olive oil

- pinch of salt

Add the roughly chopped cucumbers, avocado, arugula, parsley, garlic, lemon juice, jalapeno, olives, olive oil and salt to a bowl and mix.

Sample recipe 3

Sauteed garlic and tomato lentil salad

INGREDIENTS

- 1 cup dry green (brown) lentils
- 1/2 cup dry light bulgur (light just refers to the coarseness of the grain)
- 3–4 cups fresh tomatoes, chopped
- 6–8 cloves garlic, minced
- 2 tablespoons olive oil
- 1/2 cup parsley very finely chopped.
- 1/4 cup citrus/vinaigrette dressing
- salt and pepper to taste
- fresh lemon juice to taste.

INSTRUCTIONS

1. Cook the lentils and the bulgur according to directions, using vegetable broth instead of water. When cooked, combine, and set aside.

2. Sauté the tomatoes, garlic, and olive oil over low heat for 15 minutes or until the tomatoes and garlic are soft and fragrant.

Remove from heat. Add the lentils, bulgur, and parsley to the pan and stir to combine.

3. Season with dressing, salt and pepper, and lemon juice. Serve hot or cold.

NOTES

The lemon dressing just happened to be something I had on hand, so I tossed it in there to keep things flavorful. Any kind of oil or vinegar-based sauce or dressing that you have on hand could work for this one!

Sample recipe 4

Mixed berry smoothie for breakfast

INGREDIENTS

- ½ cup vanilla yogurt
- 2 cups mixed berries frozen
- 1 tablespoon chia seeds
- 1 cup milk/ could be coconut milk/oat milk/almond.

INSTRUCTIONS

1. Add yogurt, berries, chia seeds and milk to blender.
2. Blend until smooth.
3. Serve immediately.

SLEEP CATCHER

30-Day Sleep Routine

This plan is to get you into a good sleep routine or schedule. This is a 30-day sleep program. This program stacks habits on each other to ensure novelty. Circadian rhythm is the internal clock our bodies function on. For this internal clock to function optimally our bodies need fifteen minutes of direct sunshine, preferably between sunrise and noon. The important part remains picking a time to go to bed and no screens in the hour before sleep. This program can be adjusted to suit individual needs.

WEEK 1

Pick a bedtime. Let's say 10pm.

STEP 1

Your last meal should be completed by 8 pm.

If there are exercises in your routine, it should be relaxing like yin yoga or slow and relaxing. body movement

STEP 2

No screens after 9pm, meditate, read a book in incandescent light (from a bedside lamp)

STEP 3

Keep the room dark and cool.

WEEK 2

STEP 1

The last meal should be completed by 8 pm.

If there are exercises in your routine, it should be relaxing like yin yoga or slow and relaxing body movement.

STEP 2

No screens after 9pm, meditate, read a book in incandescent light (from a bedside lamp)

STEP 3

Keep the room dark and cool.

ACTION STEP

Add white or brown noise or binaural beats for sleep. If using an app on the phone, place phone facing downwards to eliminate blue light which disrupts the sleep routine.

OR drink chamomile tea with honey.

WEEK 3

STEP 1

The last meal should be completed by 8 pm.

If there are exercises in your routine, it should be relaxing like yin yoga or slow and relaxing body movement.

STEP 2

No screens after 9pm, meditate, read a book in incandescent light (from a bedside lamp)

STEP 3

Keep the room dark and cool.

ACTION STEP

Try a cooling sleep cap if your partner prefers the temperature at toasty.

OR add a low dose over-the-counter Melatonin or valerian root.

WEEK 4

STEP 1

The last meal should be completed by 8 pm.

If there are exercises in your routine, it should be relaxing like yin yoga or slow and relaxing body movement.

STEP 2

No screens after 9pm, meditate, read a book in incandescent light (from a bedside lamp).

STEP 3

Keep the room dark and cool.

ACTION STEP

Add Magnesium Glycinate supplement.

OR a lavender bath/ a few drops of pure lavender oil on sheets or pillowcases.

**If you are already on prescription sleep medication, consult your doctor before adding any supplements suggested in this program.

ABOUT THE AUTHOR

Born in Cameroon, West Africa, and immigrated to the United States as a teenager, Georgette Nkwo has a bachelor's degree in nursing, and currently holds a position in Case Management. Moving from a more holistic society, Cameroon, to the United States was a tremendous change and challenge, especially when it came to food and nutrition, and other non-conventional ways of dealing with health and ailments. Nevertheless, living in the USA and diving deep into a new culture widened her world view. She began learning how to live in the grey areas of life, enduring transitions from college graduate to working nurse, motherhood, and now entrepreneurship. All great achievements, yes, but not without tremendous sacrifice, some of which took a toll on her physically, mentally, and spiritually.

Coming back to my body is a journey of self-mastery told through the author's experiences on how a frightening health crisis led her to achieve balance in her body, mind, and soul. She shares her story in hopes of helping others find themselves again.

Ms. Georgette works as a Progress Catalyst, Nurse consultant and Speaker.

Contact the author at www.evolvefulness.com
Social Media Handles
Instagram: evolvefulness
TikTok: evolvefulness

Made in the USA
Monee, IL
28 July 2023

39963086R00077